# Creation's Praise

By Vivian May Edwards
Illustrated by Janis Lee Colón

Copyright © 2007 by Vivian May Edwards. 27080-EDWA
Library of Congress Control Number: 2007901927

ISBN:   Softcover   978-1-4257-6231-5
        Hardcover  978-1-4257-6264-3

CREATION'S PRAISE
PUBLISHED BY XLIBRIS CORPORATION
International Plaza II, Suite 340
Philadelphia PA 19113
*A strategic partner of Random House Ventures*

All Scripture quotations, unless otherwise indicated, are taken from the Holy Bible, New International version®. Copyright © 1973, 1978, 1984 by International Bible Society. Used by permission of Zondervan Publishing House. All rights reserved. Scripture quotations marked (KJV) are taken from the King James Version.

All rights reserved. No part of this book may be reproduced or transmitted in any form or by any means, electronic or mechanical, including photocopying, recording, or by any information storage and retrieval system, without permission in writing from the copyright owner.

This book was printed in the United States of America.

To order additional copies of this book, contact:
Xlibris Corporation
1-888-795-4274
www.Xlibris.com
Orders@Xlibris.com

# Creation's Praise

**For:** My Mother, Sarah, who lovingly led me to a saving knowledge of the Lord Jesus Christ, as a very young child and to my pastor and his wife, Dr. and Mrs. Michael Youssef, whose messages and stirring book, "Empowered by Praise", so inspired me in the writing of this devotional. Together, their godliness and spiritual example, so faithfully remind me of the amazing power of thanking and praising God in all circumstances of life.

*Thank you, Mom, Dr. Youssef and Elizabeth,*
*Blessings Forever,*
*Vivian*

*Praise the LORD. Praise the LORD from the heavens, praise him in the heights above.*
*Praise him, all his angels, praise him, all his heavenly hosts.*
*Praise him, sun and moon, praise him, all you shining stars.*
*Praise him, you highest heavens and you waters above the skies.*
*Let them praise the name of the LORD, for he commanded and they were created. He set them in place for ever and ever; he gave a decree that will never pass away.*
*Praise the LORD from the earth, you great sea creatures and all ocean depths,*
*Lightning and hail, snow and clouds, stormy winds that do his bidding,*
*you mountains and all hills, fruit trees and all cedars,*
*wild animals and all cattle, small creatures and flying birds,*
*kings of the earth and all nations, you princes and all rulers on earth,*
*young men and maidens, old men and children.*
*Let them praise the name of the LORD, for his name alone is exalted; his splendor is above the earth and the heavens. He has raised up for his people a horn, the praise of all his saints, of Israel, the people close to his heart.*
*Praise the LORD.*

*(Psalm 148:1–14)*

**Note to Adults:**

This book is intended as a tool to help you introduce your precious little ones to the great, universal symphony of praise. The King of all creation inhabits, tabernacles, pitches His tent in the praises of His people, both large and small. Encourage your children to come into God's presence with singing. Lead them by example, so that they may truly know God's wonderful blessing and comfort. My hope is that they will experience His awesome and transforming power in every area of their lives.

This devotional, can be adjusted by you to make this special time as simple or as challenging as you'd like, depending on the age and development of your child. In the discussion section you will find new vocabulary, spiritual truths, and verses that will provide opportunities for your children to praise and thank God for His names, character, and ministry in their lives.

Thank you so much for inviting me into your life! It is a privilege for me to minister to you and your children through my book. My hope and prayer is that God will be honored and glorified, and you and your children will discover the blessings of knowing the Lord Jesus as your Best Friend and Savior.

I pray your little ones will come to treasure this book, as they grasp the idea of who God is and how special they are to Him. As you and your children join in this magnificent chorus of praise to God in every circumstance of life, you will grow closer to our wonderful Lord and Savior, Jesus Christ. He loves you and your little ones so tenderly and eternally. He alone deserves every ounce of our glory, honor, and praise.

Ever and always!

*Vivian May Edwards*

*For all you special adults, who belong to these precious children....*

## PICTURE THIS

Picture this, the host of all heaven
Along with their heavenly bodies, a throng
With passion and pleasure, their songs of endearment
Of praise to the Father, enduring, so strong,
Join billions of creatures and all of creation
Who love and adore Him, Christ Jesus the King,
With highest regards for the praised Holy Spirit,
They shine with His majesty, tributes they bring.
The thought of this picture, breathtakingly true,
Should cause all God's children, yes me and yes you,
To join in this chorus of splendor and praise
And worship and honor the Father always,
To worship and honor the Father with praise

*Great is the LORD and most worthy of praise;
his greatness no one can fathom.
(Psalm 145:3)*

We listen in wonder, sweet music we hear,
The sounds of creation ring loudly, so clear.
Her songs are amazing, so lovingly sweet;
Come with us; come listen to this special treat.

*Let everything that has breath praise the LORD.*
*Praise the LORD.*
*(Psalm 150:6)*

## LET'S TALK ABOUT

| | |
|---|---|
| *Creation:* | All the things that God has made. |
| *Create:* | To make. |
| *Praise:* | To enjoy God! To tell God how wonderful He is and that you love Him very much. |
| *The Most High God:* | The God above all creation |

Praise God, as the Most High God!
Thank you, God, for all the wonderful things You have created.

God wants you to praise Him everyday.
God made you, and He loves you. He wants you to be part of His family.

*I will extol the LORD at all times;*
*his praise will always be on my lips.*
*(Psalm 34:1)*

My soft kitty cat with her gentle meow,
Her purring so soothing, consider her now.
She's praising so tenderly, so all can hear
Especially those who to her are so dear.

My precious puppies who bark with glad cheer
Sing loud, so the Savior will always hear
Their howl, so delightful, so grand and so deep
Adds overwhelming praise so sweet.

*Sing to the LORD a new song;*
*sing to the LORD, all the earth.*
*(Psalm 96:1)*

## LET'S TALK ABOUT

*Overwhelming:* To feel wonder or amazement.
*Savior:* Someone who rescues or saves people from death or danger.

Praise Jesus as the kind Savior of the world!
Thank you, Jesus, for loving me so much.

Jesus wants all the little children to come to Him.
Jesus loves each person, including you and me!

*Jesus said, "Let the little children come to me, and do not hinder them, for the kingdom of heaven belongs to such as these."*
(Matthew 19:14)

Participating with pageant, such charm
Parading, the creatures on the noisy farm.
The nay and the baaa, the oink and the quack
Pay tribute to God; they will just not hold back.

The chicken's warm clucking, the rooster's kind crow
It's just as if they all truly know
The Author of life, Elohim, Most High God
To Him, all creation gives worship and laud.

*All the earth bows down to you;*
*they sing praise to you,*
*they sing praise to your name.*
(Psalm 66:4)

## LET'S TALK ABOUT

*Tribute:* To give praise and honor to God.
*Worship:* To serve and obey God, because you love Him.
*Laud:* To praise and worship God.
*Elohim* God the Father, Son and Holy Spirit, who created everything.

Praise Elohim, the God of all creation!
Thank you, God, for creating me and giving me life.

God created you and me, for He made everything.
God is all-powerful, for He made heaven and earth.

*In the beginning God created the heavens and the earth.*
*(Genesis 1:1)*

What great joy so sweet, as the winged insect's kiss,
This orchestra softly with grandeur and bliss
With jewels so resplendent for God the Most High
He's blessed, while He reigns from His throne in the sky.

The bee family's buzzing, their songs know no end,
Vibrating their messages, tributes they send
Reminding the world, God's forever, for keeps,
No, He never slumbers, nor tires, nor sleeps.

*"Be still, and know that I am God;*
*I will be exalted among the nations,*
*I will be exalted in the earth."*
(Psalm 46:10)

## LET'S TALK ABOUT

*Grandeur:* Rich, important, big, great.
*Bliss:* To be happy and joyful.
*Resplendent:* Wonderful, bright, and great.
*Eternal:* Forever. There is no end.

Praise God because He is eternal!
Thank you, God, for always listening to me.

There is no one greater than the Most High God!
God loves you and will always keep you close to Him.

*For you, O LORD, are the Most High over all the earth;*
*you are exalted far above all gods.*
(Psalm 97:9)

Fireflies, with their codes of delight
Of awe for Christ Jesus, His heavenly light;
Of praise for His wonderful love for mankind,
There's no greater love, than His love, you will find.

Cicadas and crickets reach heavenly heights
While adding new luster to warm summer nights.
The hoot owl repeats, "God is good, God is love,"
While night creatures praise Him, who reigns up above.

*Like your name, O God,*
*your praise reaches to the ends of the earth;*
*your right hand is filled with righteousness.*
*(Psalm 48:10)*

### LET'S TALK ABOUT

| | |
|---|---|
| Awe: | To be amazed and surprised. |
| Luster: | To shine and to sparkle. |
| Reign: | To rule and have control over a group of people. |

Praise God because He is good all the time!
Thank you, Jesus, for loving me and for being so good to me.

Jesus loves you, for He loves everyone.
God is in control of you, for He is in control of everything!

*This is how we know what love is:*
*Jesus Christ laid down his life for us.*
*(1 John 3:16a)*

Even God's creatures, annoying, so pesky,
Like scorpions, spiders, mosquitoes, so testy,
Including the gnats and the fleas and the flies
Raise praises in unison up to the skies.

*Be exalted, O God, above the heavens;
let your glory be over all the earth.*
(Psalm 57:5)

## LET'S TALK ABOUT

*Unison:* To be as one.
*Exalted:* To be placed high above everyone else.
*Glory:* Beauty and brightness.

Praise God because He is beautiful and bright!
Thank you, God, for everything.

God made everything and saw that it was good!
God made you, and you are very special to Him.

*How many are your works, O LORD!*
*In wisdom you made them all;*
*the earth is full of your creatures.*
*(Psalm 104:24)*

## LET'S TALK ABOUT

*Perfection:*         To never sin or do anything wrong.
*Refuge:*            A place that protects from danger.
*Heaven:*           God's home. Where God lives.
*Holy:*               To never sin or do anything wrong.

Praise God because He is perfect and holy!
Thank you, God, for loving me even though I am not perfect.

Heaven is a perfect place, sin can never be allowed there.
God loves you, and He wants you to be in heaven with Him one day.

*As for God, his way is perfect;*
*the word of the LORD is flawless.*
*He is a shield for all who take refuge in him.*
*(2 Samuel 22:31)*

**LET'S TALK ABOUT**

*Sin:* When we disobey God. When we want our own way.
*Separation:* To be all by yourself, without anyone.
*Hell:* A dark place of suffering and sadness. Where the devil will live forever with unbelievers.

Praise Jesus as the Way, the Truth, and the Life!
Thank you, God, for loving me and wanting me to be Your child.

The punishment for sin is death and separation from God, forever, in hell.
God has a wonderful plan so that you will not have to be punished for your sin!

*For the wages of sin is death, but the gift of God is eternal life
in Christ Jesus our Lord.
(Romans 6:23)*

**LET'S TALK ABOUT**

*Jesus:*                  God's one and only Son.
*Forgive:*               To not see our sins anymore

Praise Jesus because He forgives all our sins!
Thank you, Jesus, for listening to me and forgiving me of all my sins.

You are a sinner; everyone has sinned. No one is perfect like Jesus.
Tell God that you have sinned, and He will forgive you.

*For all have sinned and fall short of the glory of God*
*(Romans 3:23)*

Continually praising, bright angels with wings
Amazed at God's grace for His loved human beings
Give high hallelujahs to Jesus the light
Who sacrificed all; what a wonderful sight!

*The heavens praise your wonders, O LORD,
your faithfulness too, in the assembly of the holy ones.
(Psalm 89:5)*

**LET'S TALK ABOUT**

*Sacrifice:* To give up something very special for someone else.
*Believe:* Being sure that something is true.

Praise God because He gave us the best gift ever—Jesus!
Thank you, Jesus, for giving up Your life for me on the cross.

God gave His Son, Jesus, so that you could have eternal life in heaven!
Jesus wants to be your Savior, to save you from all your sins.

*For God so loved the world that he gave his one and only Son,
that whoever believes in him shall not perish
but have eternal life.
(John 3:16)*

With great Latin flavor, they praise Christ the King,
Adding beat to their step, so excited, they sing.
The parrots' remarkable chatter and cheer
Praise Christ the Redeemer, who's always so near.

*Then I heard every creature in heaven and on earth
and under the earth and on the sea,
and all that is in them singing
(Revelation 5:13a)*

## LET'S TALK ABOUT

Redeemer: One who pays the full price for something.
Pure: To be clean and fresh, without sin.
Wages: The price of something.

Praise Jesus as the Pure Redeemer of the world!
Thank you, Jesus, for dying on the cross to pay for all my sins.

Jesus shed His blood and died on the cross to pay for all your sins.
Your sins will be forgiven if you believe in Jesus.

*And without the shedding of blood there is no forgiveness.*
*(Hebrews 9:22a)*

The hummingbird, vibrating so sure,
Repeating the phrase, "God is good, God is pure."
Her rushing high note of quick speed and swift flight
Brings God, the true Father, pure dazzling delight.

The butterfly, what a show, what a sight,
When transformed from a larva, to a beauty in flight
Shows off God's great power to change and to clean
Each sinner so lost, to God's splendor unseen.

*My mouth will speak in praise of the LORD.
Let every creature praise his holy name for ever and ever.
(Psalm 145:21)*

## LET'S TALK ABOUT

*Transformed:*     To change.
*Larva:*     A baby butterfly.
*Splendor:*     To be grand and glorious.
*Faith:*     To believe and trust in something.

Praise God for His changing and cleansing power!
Thank you, God, that You can change hearts to believe in Jesus.

God's gift is eternal life in heaven when you believe in Jesus.
Believe in Jesus to be cleansed from your sin and you will be saved!

*For it is by grace you have been saved, through faith—and this not from yourselves, it is the gift of God*
*(Ephesians 2:8)*

The trees of the forest, the jungles and land
Praise God for His wisdom, His great perfect plan.
So humbled are they that Christ died on a tree
So people, by faith, could be saved, could be free.

The flowers ring out with their fragrant bouquet
Reminding the world, to believe, He's the Way.
With voices like ringing bells raised to the sky,
Aromas so sweet rise to God the Most High.

*Let the fields be jubilant, and everything in them.
Then all the trees of the forest will sing for joy
(Psalm 96:12)*

## LET'S TALK ABOUT

*Truth:* What is real, true, and right.

Praise God, who gave the gift of eternal life!
Thank you, Jesus, for helping me put my faith and trust in You.

Believe in Jesus, who died to save you because He loves you.
You can be sure that you will go to heaven one day if you believe in Jesus.

*Believe in the Lord Jesus, and you will be saved*
*(Acts 16:31a)*

The woodlands, complete with God's creatures so sweet,
A standing ovation, they rise to their feet.
The squirrel and skunk and the shy, gentle deer
Know Jesus concerns Himself; they see His tear.

*Sing for joy, O heavens, for the LORD has done this;
shout aloud, O earth beneath.
Burst into song, you mountains,
you forests and all your trees*
(Isaiah 44:23a)

## LET'S TALK ABOUT

*Care:* To look after, watch over, protect.
*Concern:* A matter that is important to someone.

Praise Jesus because He cares for you!
Thank you, Jesus, for always taking care of me.

Jesus loves and cares for you all the time.
Jesus cared enough to die for your sin.

*Cast all your anxiety on him because he cares for you.*
*(1 Peter 5:7)*

The birds seem so lively, new hope on their wing
They sing of God's mercy; they praise Christ the King.
In joins the kind, peaceful, cooing, sweet dove
With melodies right from God's heaven above.

*Worship the LORD in the splendor of his holiness;*
*tremble before him, all the earth.*
*(Psalm 96:9)*

## LET'S TALK ABOUT

*Hope:* To know that God will take care of you.
*Mercy:* When someone is kind to you.


Praise Jesus because He is merciful!
Thank you, Jesus, for always being so kind to me.

God is merciful, and He will always take care of you.
Jesus gave us hope when He rose from the grave!

*The Lord is full of compassion and mercy.*
*(James 5:11b)*

The robin, so merry, so tender she'll sing
Gives praise and all glory to Jesus, the King.
Her recital is different; it's not quite the norm,
She saves her adoring note just for the storm.

*Shout for joy to the LORD, all the earth,
burst into jubilant song with music
(Psalm 98:4)*

**LET'S TALK ABOUT**

*Merry:* To be happy.
*Recital:* A musical show.
*Adoring:* To love and worship.

Praise Jesus as the King of kings and the Lord of lords!
Thank you, Jesus, for helping me when I am afraid.

Praise and trust in Jesus even when you are scared.
Jesus is the King, for He is living today!

When I am afraid, I will trust in you.
In God, whose word I praise,
in God I trust; I will not be afraid.
(Psalm 56:3–4a)

So clever, the pelican, lovely in flight
As he circles and dives for his meal, what a sight!
Adds grace, with perfection, to God's praise at sea;
God's thrilled at his hearty, soul-filled harmony.

The seaweed that houses sea babies so snug
Shows off God's surrounding sweet kiss and great hug.
He's praised for His sheltering, rescuing ways,
Adored as Protector, yes that's why they praise.

*Praise the LORD from the earth,*
*you great sea creatures and all ocean depths*
*(Psalm 148:7)*

## LET'S TALK ABOUT

*Deliver:* To set free, help, and save.
*Protector:* A person who guards against harm or danger.

Praise God as your Hiding Place!
Thank you, God, for hiding me when I need help.

God will always surround you with His love and protection.
God will put a happy song in your heart if you ask Him to.

*You are my hiding place; you will protect me from trouble
and surround me with songs of deliverance.*
(Psalm 32:7)

Waterfalls, rushing continuous with sound,
Praise God that there's more, no, His end won't be found.
He's ever abiding, the pure flowing fount,
The rainforest sings, all God's blessings they count.

Volcanoes provide a grand, awesome display
Of fireworks, lighting the sky, night and day.
Her loud booming sound radiates, God be praised!
God's constant, compassionate, ever, always.

*Let the rivers clap their hands,*
*let the mountains sing together for joy;*
*let them sing before the LORD*
(Psalm 98:8–9a)

## LET'S TALK ABOUT

*Ever abiding:*         God is always with you.
*Constant:*         To always be there for you.
*Compassionate:*         To be kind and to care about others.

Praise God for always being compassionate and kind!
Thank you, God, for always being with me.

God is eternal, for He has no beginning and no end.
God wants you to always be kind to others.

*Now to the King eternal, immortal, invisible, the only God,
be honor and glory for ever and ever. Amen.
(1 Timothy 1:17)*

The heartland, where buffalo roam free for miles,
Great Plains with her powwows, her praises, her smiles
Sound forth, God's the center of all, everything,
The Lord God Almighty, triumphantly King.

Propelling their voices, the eagles ring clear
Of praise for the Savior, His freedom so dear,
Saluting American creatures can see
God's King of this great land of grand liberty.

*Be exalted, O God, above the heavens,
and let your glory be over all the earth.*
(Psalm 108:5)

## LET'S TALK ABOUT

*Triumphantly:*                 To be on the winning team.
*Lord:*                         A person who rules.

Praise the Lord God Almighty as King over all the earth!
Thank you, God, for America—the land of the free and the brave.

Jesus Christ is King and Lord of all!
You can tell Jesus that you love Him anytime.

*That at the name of Jesus every knee should bow,*
*in heaven and on earth and under the earth,*
*and every tongue confess that Jesus Christ is Lord,*
*to the glory of God the Father.*
*(Philippians 2:10–11)*

## LET'S TALK ABOUT

*Holy Spirit:*    God's Spirit who works in and around our lives.
*Joyful:*    To feel very glad and happy.
*Trust:*    To believe and to depend on someone.

Praise God, His Son, Jesus, and the Holy Spirit, as the one true God!
Thank you, God, for helping me to laugh and to be joyful.

God will fill you with joy and peace, as you trust in Him.
God wants you to trust Him for everything you need.

*May the God of hope fill you with all joy and peace,
as you trust in him
(Romans 15:13a)*

The tribes on safari, abundant and free,
So joyful that Jesus the Savior they see.
With thankful and unified hearts, they rejoice
Applauding fantastically, with one great voice.

With chuckle and laughter, the hyenas add
The sound of rejoicing, no, no one is sad.
They join unexpected, when needed, you see;
Praise God and His Son and His Spirit, all three.

*The wild animals honor me, the jackals and the owls,
because I provide water in the desert
and streams in the wasteland
(Isaiah 43:20a)*

From over yonder, the praise down under
Explodes, with a brilliant, magnificent voice.
The kangaroo, dingo, and cockatoo lead,
While the others extol God, who meets every need.

Come see this exceptional grand celebration
So vivid with color and praise to the King,
Koalas and bilbies and emus adore Him,
Burst forth with their worship, rich tributes they bring.

*Praise the LORD, all his works everywhere in his dominion.*
*Praise the LORD, O my soul.*
*(Psalm 103:22)*

## LET'S TALK ABOUT

*Extol:* To praise and honor God.
*Provide:* To supply everything that is needed.

Praise God as Jehovah-Jireh!
Thank you, God, for giving me everything I need, all the time.

Jehovah-Jireh sees ahead and always provides for your every need!
God wants you to talk to Him every day.

*And my God will meet all your needs
according to his glorious riches in Christ Jesus.
(Philippians 4:19)*

In the jungles of Asia, all critters and beasts
Resound, and the glorious rhythms increase;
Percussions so mellow, the orchestra's lush,
While clapping before God, they come to a hush.

Included, the brass, all the elephants blow,
Excitement compels them, they know that God knows.
God knows all about them, He knows everything,
He's wise beyond measure, yes, that's why they sing.

*Praise be to his glorious name forever;*
*may the whole earth be filled with his glory.*
*Amen and Amen.*
(Psalm 72:19)

**LET'S TALK ABOUT**

Wise: To understand and know about lots of things.
Wisdom: Knowing how to use what you know.

Praise God as the God of all wisdom and knowledge!
Thank you, God, for knowing all about me.

God knows about you, for He knows everything.
God wants you to quietly listen to Him everyday.

*My frame was not hidden from you when I was made in the secret place.
When I was woven together in the depths of the earth
(Psalm 139:15)*

The Middle East, singing with Biblical flair,
Sings out in amazement, with honor and care.
They praise the Good Shepherd to whom they belong
And boast of His goodness while singing their song.

Desert creatures, some strong and some weak,
Exist for God's glory, His praises to speak.
With swift repetition the enchanting gazelle
Sings out, "God is peace, and with Him all is well."

*Let them praise the name of the LORD, for his name alone is exalted;
his splendor is above the earth and the heavens.*
(Psalm 148:13)

**LET'S TALK ABOUT**

*Shepherd:* A person who leads, protects, and watches over his sheep or a group of people
*The Good Shepherd:* The Lord Jesus Christ

Praise Jesus as the Good Shepherd!
Thank you, Jesus, for watching over me. Help me to follow You.

Jesus is your leader; He will tenderly watch over you.
God wants you to read the Bible, and pray everyday.

*The LORD is my shepherd, I shall not be in want.*
(Psalm 23:1)

The Jewel of the Nile, so amazingly grand,
Magnificent praise comes from this ancient land.
Her royal announcements resound through the year,
Reminding the world, Christ's return is so near.

*Shout with joy to God, all the earth!
Sing the glory of his name; make his praise glorious!
(Psalm 66:1-2)*

### LET'S TALK ABOUT

| | |
|---|---|
| *Salvation:* | When Jesus died, was buried, and rose again to save all people who would believe in Him, from their sin. |
| *Christ's return:* | Jesus is coming back very soon for all His children who believe in Him. |

Praise Jesus as the one true Savior of the world!
Thank you, Jesus, that You will come back for me one day.

Jesus came and will return for everyone who believes in Him.
God wants you to tell others about Jesus.

*Salvation is found in no one else, for there is no other name under heaven
given to men by which we must be saved.
(Acts 4:12)*

The rainbow sings colorful notes, bright and pure,
Forever assuring, God's promise is sure.
Projecting God's comfort, His hope strong and true;
Why people don't trust Him, I haven't a clue.

The breeze, her gentle whispers say,
"With joy, I'll give Him my display
Of praise forever, for His love
Yes, while He rules from heaven above."

And the heavens proclaim his righteousness,
for God himself is judge.
(Psalm 50:6)

## LET'S TALK ABOUT

*Promise:* To say that you will do something a certain way for sure.
*Comfort:* When you feel calm or peaceful.

Praise God as the God of Truth!
Thank you, God, for always keeping Your promises.

God doesn't lie. He will always keep His promises.
God wants you to learn all about His promises from His word.

*The LORD is faithful to all his promises*
*and loving toward all he has made.*
*(Psalm 145:13b)*

Storm clouds performing, with great admiration,
Add depth and respect to this praise celebration.
Informing creation in God they can trust
When darkness surrounds them, their world's 'bout to bust.

Even the thunder and lightning the same,
With loud, clashing voices proclaim God's great name.
Their bright, flashy cymbals will bring up the rear,
Highlighting God's essence, His holiness dear.

*Lightning and hail, snow and clouds, stormy winds that do his bidding …*
*Let them praise the name of the LORD*
*(Psalm 148:8, 13a)*

## LET'S TALK ABOUT

*Admiration:* To feel that someone is very special.
*Essence:* The real part of someone; the spirit.

Praise God because He is trustworthy!
Thank you, God, that I can always trust You when I am afraid.

The Bible is God's word, and every word in the Bible is true!
Jesus wants to be your best friend.

> *In God I trust; I will not be afraid.*
> *What can man do to me?*
> *(Psalm 56:11)*

The clouds so fluffy, so bright with delight,
Add pure celebration, expressing God's light;
Adding joy and excitement, applause without end,
When praise to the Father, the fluffy clouds send.

The sky so blue, filled with mercies brand new,
Each morning pursues God and shows off He's true,
For His love never changes nor comes to an end,
Yes, the clouds and the sky harmonize; what a blend!

*Sing to God, sing praise to his name, extol him who rides on the clouds—*
*his name is the LORD—and rejoice before him.*
*(Psalm 68:4)*

## LET'S TALK ABOUT

*Celebration:*      A party or holiday in honor of someone.

Praise God as the Father of the heavenly lights!
Thank you, God, for Your mercy and for every beautiful, new day.

God is light, for He is always the same and He never changes!
God wants you to have a happy heart as you trust in Him.

*Every good and perfect gift is from above,
coming down from the Father of the heavenly lights,
who does not change like shifting shadows.
(James 1:17)*

Sunrise, when darkness dies, morning has come,
Breaking the silence, God's creatures wake, hum.
Yes, eager sweet voices, with happy hearts too,
Praise God their Creator, for this day, brand new.

*Where morning dawns and evening fades
you call forth songs of joy.
(Psalm 65:8b)*

**LET'S TALK ABOUT**

Consumed: To be destroyed.

Praise God as your great and faithful God!
Thank you, God, for showing me Your love every morning.

God's kindness and love are new every morning!
God loves to hear your happy songs every day.

*Because of the LORD's great love we are not consumed,
for his compassions never fail.
They are new every morning; great is your faithfulness.*
(Lamentations 3:22–23)

God's master creation, each girl and each boy,
When hearing them praise Him, He's filled with great joy.
So special are they to the Savior, you see,
Heaven rejoices, when they bow the knee.

*From the lips of children and infants
you have ordained praise
(Psalm 8:2a)*

## LET'S TALK ABOUT

*Ordained:*            To choose or design

Praise God as the One who sees and hears everything!
Thank you, God, for listening to me when I praise You.

You are so special to God that He even counts every one of your hairs!
God is listening to you every day.

*And even the very hairs of your head are all numbered*
*(Matthew 10:30)*

Dear Heavenly Daddy, I'm praising You too;
I'm joining this symphony, knowing that You
Will come and receive with Your loving embrace
This praise from my heart, with a smile on Your face.

*I praise you because I am fearfully and wonderfully made;
your works are wonderful, I know that full well.
(Psalm 139:14)*

## LET'S TALK ABOUT

*Embrace:* To welcome or to give a big hug.
*Fearfully:* To be wonderful, very special, very important.
*Wonderfully:* To be good, great, and terrific.
*Inhabitest:* To dwell, in a very special way, to live in.

Praise God as your Heavenly Daddy who loves you very much!
Thank you, God, for Your hugs and for creating me to be so special.

God loves to hear you praise His name.
You can praise God anytime and anywhere.

*But thou art holy,
O thou that inhabitest the praises of Israel.
(Psalm 22:3, KJV)*

## LET'S TALK ABOUT

*Triumph:* To be very, very happy because we have won something.
*Marvelous:* To be wonderful and great.

Praise God as the Almighty King!
Thank you, God, for being so wonderful to me and to my family.

God is so wonderful that even the stones will praise Him if we don't!
God wants you to go to church, so you can learn how to please Him.

*"I tell you," he replied, "if they keep quiet,
the stones will cry out."*
*(Luke 19:40)*

Dear _____,

Thank you for reading my book. I hope you enjoyed it and learned wonderful things about God. The most important thing I wanted you to know is that Jesus loves you so much! Because of sin, and because of His love, God sent His Son, Jesus, to this world long ago to pay for that sin.

The Bible, God's Word, promises that whoever believes in Jesus, will be forgiven, will live forever in heaven with Him. And the most wonderful thing about the Bible is that every word is always true. You can believe it because God always keeps His promises.

Write to me! I love you too and hope to see you in heaven one day!

Love,

*Miss Vivian*

# Creations Praise

By Vivian May Edwards
Illustrated By Janis Lee Colòn